BELIEFS AND CULTURES

Jewish

Monica Stoppleman

FRANKLIN WATTS
NEW YORK • LONDON • SYDNEY

© 1996 Watts Books

Watts Books
96 Leonard Street
London
EC2A 4RH

Franklin Watts Australia
14 Mars Road
Lane Cove
NSW 2066

0 7496 2059 5

10 9 8 7 6 5 4 3 2

A CIP catalogue record for this book is available
from the British Library.
Dewey Decimal Classification Number 296

Series Editor: Sarah Ridley
Designer: Liz Black
Copy Editor: Nicola Barber
Consultant: Clive Lawton
Picture Researchers: Brooks Krikler
Photographer (activities): Peter Millard
Illustrators: pages 6 and 13 Aziz Khan, pages 7
and 10 Piers Harper.

Photographs:John Birdsall 26; Werner Braun 12b, 25b; Chris
Fairclough 25t; Eye Ubiquitous cover (right), 11b, 17b; Format
8b, 15, 28, 31; Judy Goldhill 16b; Sonia Halliday 14bl; Robert
Harding Picture Library 6t; David Hoffman 30br; Hutchison
Library 14tr, 20tr, 21b, 23; Hulton Deutsch 30tl; Peter Millard
24t, 29b; Network 5; Miriam Reikh 20tl; Frank Spooner Pictures
4b; Monica Stoppleman 11t, 12t, 17t, 18, 22; Trip 8t; ZEFA cover
(left), 16t (both), 21t, 29t.

With thanks to: Ruth Thomson of Thumbprint Books; Lola and
Becca Almudevar; Susan King and Prof. Mike and Sheila Billig;
Barbara, Michael and Richard Kissman and Rabbi Perez; Rabbi
Margaret Jacobi; Reni Chapman; Nottingham Rosh Chodesh
Group; George and Leigh Fenigsohn, Larry Beckreck; Sheila
Litman; Judy Goldhill for the recording of 'A Strange Legacy';
Jonothon Stock Hesketh; Lizzie Kessler; Claremont School; and
Rejina Rostance-Sachs, Oded and Jackie Shimshon, Dorry Lake,
Judy Liebert and Fred Brookes.

Printed in Great Britain

To Monica's father, Gunter Stoppleman, and to her mother, Gerdy Stoppleman, née Mannheimer, who survived the Holocaust, and to the memory of all those, including her grandparents and other relatives, who did not.

CONTENTS

WHO ARE THE JEWS? 4

THE TORAH 8

THE TEMPLE 10

THE SYNAGOGUE 12

THE JEWISH WAY OF LIFE 16

RITES OF PASSAGE 20

THE JEWISH YEAR 23

PERSECUTION OF JEWISH PEOPLE 30

GLOSSARY AND INDEX 32

Four thousand years ago, the hills and deserts of the Middle East were inhabited by many tribes of people. Today, the descendants of one of those hill tribes are still easily identifiable. They are called the Jews.

Over the centuries, Jews have dispersed to live on every continent, but many of them still practise the same religion as their ancestors. This religion is called Judaism. Jews speak the language of the countries in which they now live, and they also use Hebrew, the language of those original tribespeople, for religious

All except one of these people can lay claim to being Jewish.

Grandfather with his grandson, USA. The *Shema* prayer tells Jews to teach Judaism to their children.

purposes. Many Jews around the world base the way they live on the same holy books and pray in similar ways. They celebrate festivals and special times around the year to remind them of important events in their long history.

Many people have tried to stop the Jews being a separate group, sometimes by persuasion, but often by force. However, the Jews have held on to their beliefs and traditions, and the Jewish identity has endured for thousands of years.

WHO IS A JEW?

To be Jewish is to belong to a group - that of the Jewish people.
According to Jewish law, any person whose mother is Jewish is Jewish, whether or not he or she is religious. Some people consider themselves to be Jewish if only their father is Jewish. Jews who actively follow Judaism as a religion are called practising or observant Jews. Jews who do not are called secular Jews.

These men are *Chassidic* Jews. Their families emigrated from Eastern Europe in the 19th century to escape persecution. They still wear the traditional dress of their forefathers.

INTERVIEW

You don't have to be religious to be Jewish - it's about belonging to a social group whose unfortunate experiences have bound them together.
Gerdy Stoppleman, aged 80 New York, USA.

You can go anywhere in the world and you meet Jewish people and you're at home. You can go into any *shul* (synagogue) and know exactly what's going on. It's wonderful.
Barbara Kissman, aged 41 Nottingham, UK.

Jerusalem provides a focus for Jews, Muslims and Christians alike.

Israel is the Jewish State. It was founded in 1948 in part of the Middle East where the homeland of the Jews was in Biblical times. The capital is Jerusalem, which is a holy city for Christians and Muslims, as well as for Jews. Two main groups of people live in Israel - Jews and Arabs. The official languages are Hebrew and Arabic. Although it is only a small place, Israel is very important to Jews all over the world, as it has always played a crucial part in their history.

Counting Jews is difficult. People rely on census figures and synagogue membership. The estimate of 13 million Jews worldwide is probably on the low side. Many Jews have emigrated to Israel but the largest number of Jews lives in the United States of America.

WHERE JEWS LIVE

- Majority of Jews
- Large communities
- Smaller communities
- Scattering of Jews

THE STORY OF ABRAHAM

According to the Jewish Bible the first Jew was Abraham. When he and his wife, Sarah, were old, Abraham heard a voice telling him to leave Mesopotamia, where they lived, and journey to a land which he would be shown. This land was Israel.

The voice offered him a covenant (an agreement). If Abraham would accept this voice as God's and follow His instructions, then Abraham's descendants would become a great nation. Abraham obeyed, and what God promised came true. As the years passed, the Israelites accepted Abraham's God as the only God and considered Abraham as the father of their nation and religion.

Famine forced Abraham's grandson and family to leave Israel and go to Egypt. In Egypt, the Pharaoh (king) forced the Israelites to work as slaves. After many years of suffering, the Israelites almost forgot Abraham's God.

However, a new leader, Moses, heard the voice of God telling him to ask the Pharaoh to let the Israelites go. Time and time again the Pharaoh refused, so God sent ten plagues to punish the Egyptians. The last plague was the worst - all the first-born sons of the Egyptians died, but God passed over the houses of the Israelites and spared their sons. The grieving Pharaoh finally ordered the Israelites to go. They fled at once, but no sooner had they set out than the Pharaoh changed his mind and sent his army to bring them back. With their pursuers hot on their heels, the Israelites reached the Red Sea. They were trapped, and it seemed that there was no way across. But Moses held up his rod and the sea rolled back to make a dry path. The Israelites crossed over. When the Egyptians tried to follow, the waters rushed back, drowning them all.

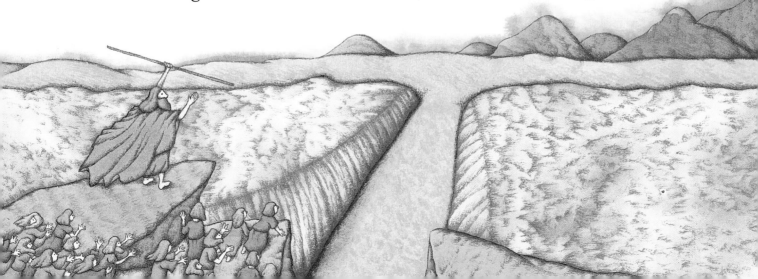

THE TORAH

A Torah scroll is treated with great respect and is often dressed in a velvet cover called a mantle, hung with a silver breastplate, a silver pointer and bells.

The Torah is handwritten on parchment scrolls by trained writers called scribes. It takes a full year to write.

The Jewish Bible tells how, after fleeing from Egypt, the Israelites wandered for many years in the desert until they came to Mount Sinai. Here, the story says, the most important event in the history of the Jews took place. God called Moses to the mountain top and gave him the *Torah* (which means 'teachings' in Hebrew) - the first five books of the Bible. These books trace the history of the Jewish people from God's creation of the world, through their flight from Egypt to their rediscovery of the land of Israel. The Torah also explains what God is like and contains the rules by which He wants His people to live.

The Jewish Bible is what Christians call the 'Old Testament'. The New Testament of the Christian Bible tells the story of Jesus of Nazareth, a Jew whom Christians believe was the Messiah. Jews do not accept this and are still hoping that the Messiah will come. As well as the Torah, the Jewish Bible contains the writings of the Prophets giving the later history of the Jews, and other holy writings, such as the Psalms. It is written mainly in Hebrew.

Ten Commandments for Today

What to do:

1 Paint a sheet of cardboard pale grey all over. Cut it into the shape of a stone tablet.

2 Write down the ten most important rules that you think might help people get along together in the modern world. Compare your list with your friends' lists.

> 1. You shouldn't hurt anyone on purpose.
> 2. You should share things with other people.
> 3.
> 4.
> 5.
> 6.
> 7.
> 8.
> 9.
> 10.

THE TEN COMMANDMENTS

God's ten most important commandments were brought down from the mountain by Moses, engraved on two tablets of stone. Today, the rules of many legal systems in the world are based upon them.

1 I am the Lord your God who brought you out of slavery in Egypt.
2 You shall have no other gods besides Me. You must not make any idols to bow down to or worship.
3 You shall not misuse the name of the Lord your God.
4 Remember to keep the Sabbath day holy and not do any work on it.
5 Respect your father and mother, so that you may live long in the land the Lord your God is giving you.
6 You must not murder.
7 You must not commit adultery.
8 You must not steal.
9 You must not give false evidence against your neighbour.
10 You must not be envious of your neighbour's house nor his wife, nor anything that belongs to your neighbour.

THE TEMPLE

The Torah tells us that the stone tablets with the Ten Commandments written on them were kept in a golden box called the Ark of the Covenant. The Israelites carried this box with them wherever they went. After Moses died, they entered their promised land - Israel. Their king, David, made Jerusalem its centre of worship. Solomon, his son, built a temple to house the Ark.

The Jews worshipped there for hundreds of years until Israel was conquered by the Babylonians. The Temple was destroyed and many Jews were taken into exile in Babylon. Eventually a new Temple was built on the same site. This was destroyed by the Romans, who drove the Jews out of their land. The Jews scattered over the world and have mourned the destruction of their Temple ever since.

This is how the second Temple may have looked. Only men were allowed in the inner courtyard.

REBUILDING THE TEMPLE

Many Jews believe that the Temple was the holiest place in the world. They look forward to a time when the Temple will be rebuilt for a third time, and everyone will go there to worship God. They believe this will happen when the Messiah comes. The Messiah will be a leader whom God will send to bring peace all over the world. The Temple is mentioned in many of the daily Jewish prayers.

The *ner tamid* lamp is never allowed to go out, to show that God is ever-present.

The Western Wall in Jerusalem is part of the boundary wall of the old Temple. Jews come here from all over the world to recite prayers.

THE SYNAGOGUE

The synagogue of an Orthodox congregation. Synagogues vary widely.

In an Orthodox synagogue, such as this one in Jerusalem, Israel, men and women sit separately.

Many Jews believe that it is important to pray to God. Prayers are said at events that happen in the home, but some prayers must be said in the company of other Jews. For these prayers and readings from the Torah, Jews go to a building called a *synagogue*. This is a community centre used for study and celebration as well as for prayer.

Synagogues vary in size and shape. Some are small and hidden away. Others are large and imposing. They are often built in the local style of architecture. Most synagogues are built to face towards Jerusalem, where the Temple stood. Members pay towards the upkeep of the synagogue. Not every one who attends synagogue is a member.

SPOTLIGHT
There are different ways of practising Judaism. For instance: •Orthodox and Conservative Jews do things by the book - the book being the Jewish Codes of Law. •Reform and Progressive Jews think that Jewish beliefs and practices can be developed and changed.

INSIDE A SYNAGOGUE

The inside of every synagogue is based on the Temple.
Many synagogues have separate rooms for study and
teaching children, a hall for social gatherings, a kitchen
for preparing food and a library.

Orthodox Synagogue

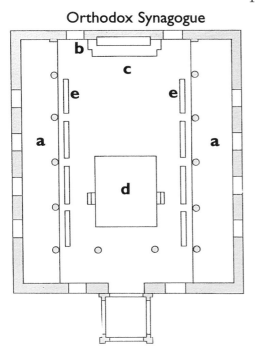

Reform Synagogue

a Women's gallery
and seats
b The Ark
c The ner tamid
d The bimah
e Seats

AN ORTHODOX SYNAGOGUE

In an Orthodox synagogue the men
sit downstairs and are called up to
the *bimah* (platform) to read from
the scrolls and open the Ark doors.
The women follow the service in a
separate section of the synagogue,
often an upstairs gallery. The service
is conducted in Hebrew. In the
Orthodox synagogue a *minyan*
(ten men) is necessary for public
religious worship. For some parts of
the service people stand, for the rest
of the time they sit.

A REFORM SYNAGOGUE

Men and women sit and stand
together and play an equal part in
the service. Rabbis can be male or
female. The prayers are shorter than
those in Orthodox synagogues and
some are read in the language of the
country. A minyan is not essential.

WORSHIP IN THE SYNAGOGUE

Traditionally prayers are said three times a day - in the morning, afternoon and evening. Men cover their heads with a skull-cap, as a sign of respect. At morning prayers, men wear a prayer shawl, known as a *tallit*. On weekday mornings some also wear two small boxes containing the Shema, the most important Jewish prayer. One box is tied to the forehead and the other to the left arm facing the heart. These are called *tephillin*.

This boy is wearing a tallit (prayer shawl) and tephillin (boxes), as worn at prayer.

A different portion of the Torah is read every week when Jews pray together. There are specific days when a special passage of the Torah is read. The congregation also use the *Siddur* (the Hebrew Prayer Book). Many Jews only go to the synagogue on major holy days.

The rabbi is a counsellor and teacher, helping people to understand the Torah.

THE RABBI

The religious leader and teacher of a Jewish community is called a *rabbi*. He or she has studied the Torah and Jewish law. Rabbis read and interpret God's law and guide the community in how to keep the commandments of the law in their everyday lives. Many other people are also actively involved in the service, reading, opening the Ark doors and lifting the scrolls.

This woman rabbi is teaching children about Judaism in cheder.

CHEDER

Education is considered by Jews to be extremely important. Many Jewish parents send their children to *cheder* (lessons in the synagogue) after school or on Sundays. The children learn how to read Hebrew so that they can follow the prayers. They read Bible stories, learn about Jewish history, make things for the festivals and learn Hebrew songs.

SPOTLIGHT

• The Shema is the most important Jewish prayer. Jewish children are taught to say it before they go to sleep. Observant Jews say it night and morning.

• These are the words of the beginning of the Shema: 'Hear, O Israel: the Lord is our God, the Lord is One. And you shall love the Lord your God with all your heart, with all your soul, and with all your might.'

THE HEBREW ALPHABET

Hebrew is the language in which the Bible was originally written. It has been adopted and modernised to make it the living language used in Israel today. Unlike English, it is read from right to left. A Hebrew book opens the opposite way round to a book written in English. The Hebrew alphabet has 22 letters - five of them are written slightly differently if they come at the end of a word (see bottom line). Vowels are written as little marks with the letters.

THE HEBREW ALPHABET

Read this from right to left.

L KH Y T KH Z V H D G B Silent

לכיטיחזוהדגבא

T S/SH R K TZ P/F Silent S N M

תשרקצפעסנמ

Five letters are written differently at the end of a word.

TZ P/F N M KH

ץףןםך

These words mean Happy New Year.

לשנה טובה

They are pronounced *L'Shanah Tovah*. Can you write your name in Hebrew? Remember to write from the right.

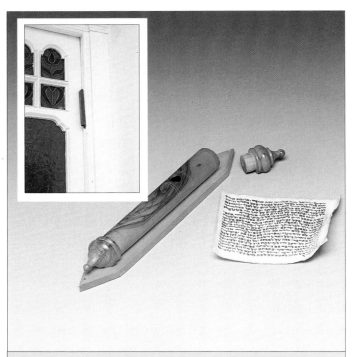

This box, called a *mezuzah,* on the doorpost of a Jewish house (inset), contains a parchment scroll on which part of a prayer, the Shema, is written.

Jewish law demands that anyone asking for charity should be given gifts.

The Torah contains rules and teachings which cover every aspect of daily life. There are 613 of these mitzvot (commandments). People who follow them are called observant Jews. The mitzvot were written long ago and some no longer apply, but Jews still believe that their basic messages hold true. Observant Jews also believe that by following these rules, they are serving God.

THE DUTIES OF A JEW

Jews believe they should try to bring out the best in themselves and others, by striving for justice, showing respect and compassion, and helping those who are sick, poor or in need. It is not considered worthy for people to seek wealth for its own sake, but to have enough to care for themselves, their families and the less fortunate. Judaism teaches that a tenth of a person's income rightfully belongs to the poor.

Keeping the body healthy and clean is the duty of a Jew. Drinking too much, smoking and taking drugs not only harms a person but also harms others around him or her.

This is a kosher kitchen. Meat and milk products are kept separate so there are two of everything - sinks, sets of plates. This woman is preparing a chicken.

INTERVIEW

Judaism is about discipline really. My family keep kosher. From when I was little I knew I had to wait a set time to have ice cream after a meaty dinner.

Ruth Goodwin, aged 14
London, UK.

Parents are expected to feed, clothe and educate their children and to teach them to be self-reliant. Children must respect their parents and teachers. Animals also have a right to proper care. If animals are killed for food, this should be done in the most painless way possible.

SPOTLIGHT

- All plants are kosher.
- No animal is considered kosher unless it has been killed in a painless way and the blood soaked out.
- Beef, lamb and venison are kosher meats.
- Pork and shellfish are not kosher.

KOSHER FOOD

Jews are commanded to keep kosher, which means 'fit or correct'. Jewish law contains some rules about what Jews should eat, and how those foods should be prepared, but nowadays few Jews keep all of them.

A kosher pizzeria in Paris.

SHABBAT

Judaism is very much about how Jews conduct their daily lives. The observance of *Shabbat*, the weekly day of rest, which lasts from Friday sunset until the first stars appear on Saturday evening, is of great importance. The Torah states: 'On six days you shall work and on the seventh you shall rest.' (Exodus)

Most Jews try to keep Shabbat as a family day, and often have a special supper on Friday night. Some people observe the commandment very strictly. They don't cook, drive, watch television, handle money or use the phone on Shabbat. They feast and rest, study and play, chat and go to the synagogue.

THE SHABBAT TABLE

On Friday evenings, the table is laid with a white cloth and the best dishes and silverware. Two candlesticks and a cup for wine are set out. On the table are two loaves of plaited bread, called *challah*. Before the meal begins the father says a special prayer with the wine, called the *Kiddush* prayer, to thank God for the gift of Shabbat, and to praise God for the challah as a gift of the earth.

Just before the sun sets, the mother of the family lights the candles and beckons in the warmth and harmony of Shabbat.

INTERVIEW

Friday nights were special. You always knew what you were going to eat - chopped liver, chicken soup with dumplings and roast chicken. Thursday was cooking day because on Friday the house had to be cleaned for Shabbat.

Barbara Kissman, aged 41, remembering Shabbat as a child

MAKING CHALLAH

WHAT TO DO:

1 Dissolve 1 tablespoon of sugar in a bowl with 125ml of warm water. Sprinkle on the yeast and whisk. Cover and leave in a warm place until it is frothy.

2 Whisk the eggs and mix with the oil, salt and 1 tablespoon of sugar in a measuring jug. Add warm water until the mixture reaches the 400ml mark on the jug.

3 Put the flour into a big bowl. Slowly add the yeast and oil mixtures. Fold in the flour with a wooden spoon.

4 Cover the bowl with a cloth and put it in a warm place. When the dough has doubled in size, knead it on a floured surface for 10 minutes. Let it rise again, before you press it down and divide into six equal lumps. Roll into six lengths. Plait the bread, following the numbers on the diagrams.

5 Place on a greased baking tray and let it rise until double in bulk. Brush with egg. Bake in the oven for 15 minutes. Reduce to 190°C (gas mark 5) and bake for another 35 minutes.

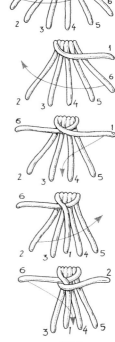

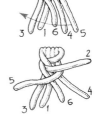

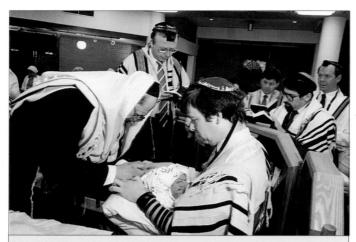

The family watches a circumcision. A trained person, called a *mohel*, performs the operation.

This boy is studying the Torah with the help of the Rabbi. He has been given his tallit for his Bar Mitzvah.

Major events in a Jewish person's life are marked by specific activities.

BRIT MILAH - CIRCUMCISION

When a baby boy is eight days old, providing he is in good health, a simple operation to remove the foreskin over the penis is carried out. The child is then blessed and named. This is a very happy and solemn occasion. Girls are named at home or in the synagogue.

BAR MITZVAH AND BAT MITZVAH

At 13, boys are considered old enough to take on adult religious responsibilities. This is marked by a ceremony called a *Bar Mitzvah*, which is their passage to adulthood. For months beforehand, a boy studies Hebrew, learning to read, and even sing, a portion of the Torah and a passage from the Prophets.

In some communities girls have a ceremony called a *Bat Mitzvah* which is like the boys' Bar Mitzvah. In others they mark their passage to adulthood at the age of 12 with a *Bat Chayil* ceremony in the synagogue. Friends and relatives listen to the boys and girls read in synagogue, and celebrate with a meal and presents.

This girl is practising the part of the Torah that she will read at her Bat Mitzvah.

MARRIAGE

According to tradition, marriage is the ideal relationship in which men and women can be fulfilled. The ceremony can take place at home or in a synagogue, but should ideally be outdoors. The groom gives the bride a ring, saying, "Be my wife according to the law of Moses and of Israel." The couple exchange wedding rings, symbolising the bond of their marriage. Traditionally, Jewish couples also exchange a *ketubah*, a marriage contract. This states the responsibilities that each person will undertake in the marriage. The couple sips from a cup of wine, and the ceremony concludes when the husband stamps on a wine glass. The joyous guests then shout "*Mazel tov!*" which means "Congratulations!"

The couple stand under a canopy, called a *chupa*. This symbolises harmony and the openness of the Jewish home.

This Jewish cemetery serves both the *Sephardi* and *Ashkenazi* communities. The Sephardi tombstones are on the left.

DEATH

Death is the natural end of life and is accepted as such. The dead body is treated with as much respect as when he or she was alive. A watcher keeps the dead body company and a candle is kept lit until the funeral, which is held as soon after death as possible. The body is washed and dressed in a simple garment. Jews are buried in plain coffins in Jewish cemeteries, without any flowers. Mourners fill the grave by shovelling in earth. After the funeral, friends and family greet the mourners with the words, "We wish you a long life," to show their concern is for the living.

MOURNING THE DEAD

A *shiva* (week of mourning) for a close relative follows the funeral. Traditionally mourners do not go out, but stay quietly at home, expressing their grief as openly as they wish. Religious services are held at the house. *Kaddish*, a special prayer praising God, is said. Friends and family bring cooked meals and remember the person who has died. For the rest of the year, prayers are said for the dead person at the synagogue. A year after the funeral, a simple tombstone is put up at a dedication ceremony, and prayers are said for the dead person on the anniverary of their death which is called the *Yahrzeit*.

The western world uses a solar calendar (based on the sun), which has 365.25 days in a year. The Jewish calendar is lunar (based on the cycles of the moon). Each month is counted from New Moon to New Moon, lasting either 29 or 30 days. Over 12 months, this adds up to 354 days. By adding an extra month seven times in 19 years, the solar and lunar calendars are brought into line. This means that the festivals occur in the same season every year.

The blowing of the *shofar* (a hollowed ram's horn) reminds Jews to repent at the time of Yom Kippur.

ROSH HASHANAH AND YOM KIPPUR

Rosh Hashanah and *Yom Kippur* are the High Holidays, the most important days of the year. They begin and end the Ten Days of Penitence, when Jews look back on any misdeeds of the year. If they have wronged someone, they are expected to put things right with that person during this time.

On Rosh Hashanah, New Year's Day, many Jews do not go to work or school. Instead they attend services at the synagogue. Traditional Jews imagine God opening an account book of reckoning. If they truly repent, he will set them down for a good year. The accounts close on Yom Kippur, the Day of Atonement, when Jews fast and pray all day. Yom Kippur is the holiest day of the Jewish year. It is the only day in the year when Jews kneel to pray.

SPOTLIGHT

- Yom Kippur is the most serious day of the Jewish Year. It is in September/October.

- *Pesach* is in March/April and celebrates the Exodus from Egypt.

On Rosh Hashanah, people share apples and honey to wish each other a sweet year. They say, "May you be written down for a good year", and they wish each other well over the Fast. Recently people have started to send each other greetings cards.

MAKING A ROSH HASHANAH CARD

YOU WILL NEED:
- *card*
- *fine black felt tip pen*
- *gold marker*
- *scissors*
- *ruler*
- *coloured pencils or felt tip pens*

WHAT TO DO:

1 Fold a piece of white card in half, keeping the fold on the right.

2 Decorate the outside with one or more of these images. Add a border.

3 Write L'Shana Tova (Happy New Year).

The sukkah is hung with fruits, paper chains and sweets.

SUKKOT

The week after Yom Kippur, some Jews build a hut roofed with leaves and branches, called a *sukkah* (plural: *sukkot*), in their gardens or at their synagogue. Some people live and eat in these sukkot for a week. *Sukkot* is a celebration of the first fruits of the harvest. People also remember the protection that God gave their ancestors about 3,600 years ago. After escaping from Egypt, the Israelites lived in sukkot in the desert, until they reached Israel.

SIMCHAT TORAH

Simchat Torah comes immediately after Sukkot. Simchat Torah means the celebration of the Torah and marks the end of the readings from the Torah scrolls. The scrolls are rolled back to the beginning, so the readings can start again. It is a time of great merriment. People take turns carrying the scrolls around the synagogue, singing songs and dancing. Children wave flags and carry candles.

During Sukkot, people pray for rain, as here at the Western Wall, holding the fruit and branches of plants that need water.

CHANUKAH

Chanukah is the mid-winter festival of lights. It celebrates a time when Jews kept the flame of their faith alight.

Two thousand years ago, the Syrian Greeks ruled the Israelites. The king, Antiochus, wanted the Jews to adopt Greek ways. Some brave Jews rebelled. They fled to the hills and formed an army, known as the Maccabees because they were led by Judah Maccabeus. After many battles the Maccabees drove the Syrians out. The Jews repaired the Temple in Jerusalem, which had been spoiled and neglected. When it was ready, they decided to hold a dedication ceremony, called Chanukah in Hebrew. However, when the Jews went to light the oil lamp which burns in front of the Ark, they found only one sealed bottle of oil - enough to last for a day. Then a miracle happened! The oil lasted until they had prepared some new oil, eight days later.

This is why the modern Chanukah celebration lasts eight nights. People remember the bravery of those who faced death rather than give up God's commandments. This is a happy festival when people have parties, eat foods fried in oil such as doughnuts and potato pancakes, play a game with a spinning top, called a *dreidel*, and receive Chanukah money.

People remember Chanukah by lighting eight candles on a *chanukiah*, also called a *menora*. Each night another candle is lit until all eight are alight.

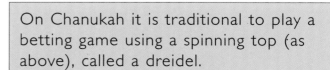

On Chanukah it is traditional to play a betting game using a spinning top (as above), called a dreidel.

Making a Chanukiah

YOU WILL NEED:

- clay
- knife
- glue
- paintbrushes
- varnish
- poster paints
- small candles
- matches

WHAT TO DO:

1 Divide in half a lump of clay the size of a small melon. Divide one of the halves into nine lumps.

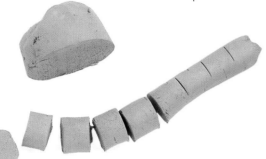

3 Shape the large lump into a long base, with wells for the eight holders. The ninth candle must stand separately from the rest. It is called a *shammash* and is used to light the other candles. Make the wells for the candles 3cm apart. While the clay is soft mark a pattern on the base.

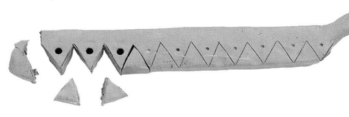

2 Shape the small lumps into nine blocks. Make a hole large enough to hold a candle in each one, using the end of a paintbrush.

4 Let it dry overnight at room temperature. Glue the holders to the base and decorate them.

27

PURIM

The word *Purim* comes from the Persian word *pur* which means a lottery or random chance. About 2,500 years ago, the Persian king, Ahasuerus, was told by his chief adviser, Haman, that his Jewish subjects were plotting against him. Haman was lying, but Ahasuerus believed him. Haman chose at random the date on which the king should order the Jews to be put to death.

At Purim, children dress up and, in some places, parade through the streets before going to a party in the synagogue.

However, Haman had overlooked the fact that the queen, Esther, was Jewish. At great risk to herself, she told the king of Haman's lies, but not before the death warrant had gone out. The king authorised the Jews to defend themselves, and they fought their enemies triumphantly.

Every year at Purim, this story is read out in the synagogue. Whenever Haman's name is mentioned, everyone boos and stamps and whirls rattles, called *greggors*.

PESACH

Pesach, called Passover in English, celebrates the Jews' escape from slavery in Egypt. It is a time when Jews thank God for their freedom. Some people spring-clean their houses to remove every crumb of leavened bread (bread containing yeast). They put away their everyday dishes and use a set of dishes kept specially for Passover.

For a week, people eat *matzot* (unleavened bread without yeast) to remind them that the Jews left Egypt in such a hurry that they could not even wait for bread to rise, and they had to make bread without yeast. On the first evening of the festival, the family gathers for a *Seder* meal, the Passover ritual. The youngest person asks 'The Four Questions'.

The answers to these questions tell the legend of the Jews' exodus from Egypt. This Passover story is told in a book called the *Haggadah*.

At different points in the story the family tastes a particular traditional food on the seder plate (see below) which symbolises the life of the Israelites in Egypt. Just before the meal is served, a matza is broken in half. This is called the *Afikoman*. One half is hidden and after the meal the children hunt for it. The finder gets a present. The rejoining of the Afikoman reminds Jews that those who are divided shall be reunited.

These people are at a Seder meal. It is customary to invite friends to join in, particularly people who might otherwise be alone.

Bitter herbs and vegetables (usually horseradish) are reminders of the misery of slavery.

The salt water reminds people of the tears of the slaves.

Karpas, parsley or lettuce, is a sign of spring, bringing hope for the future.

A roasted egg is a reminder of the destruction of the Temple and also the festival offerings made when it still stood.

A roasted bone is a reminder of the Passover sacrificial lamb that each Jewish family used to offer and eat when the Temple still stood.

Charoset is a mixture of crushed nuts, apples and wine, representing the cement used by the Israelites in building Egyptian cities.

PERSECUTION

The German Nazis rounded up men, women, children and old people alike.

By the second century CE (Common Era) the Jewish people had been driven out of Israel by the Romans. Ever since the *Diaspora*, or 'the scattering', Jews have lived in other lands. They have tried to be both loyal citizens in their new homes and to continue to follow their own traditions and religion. Jews who cease to keep either the traditions or the religion and take on the habits of people around them are called assimilated Jews.

For thousands of years, Jews have been persecuted throughout the world simply for being Jewish. This persecution is called anti-semitism. It has taken different forms at different times in different places. Laws have been made restricting where Jews can live, what work they can do, whether they can own land and whom they can marry. Many attempts, often violent, have been made to force them to accept Christianity. Refusal to do so has often meant death. Over and over again whole communities have been driven from their homes and their possessions stolen from them. Many people have been massacred. Some countries have expelled their entire Jewish populations.

By the late 19th century, some Jewish thinkers had begun to wonder

Anti-semitism continues to this day. These graves have been desecrated with swastikas, the Nazi Party symbol.

whether the Jews as a people could become independent again. Small numbers emigrated to their historic homeland, renamed Palestine.

Then a terrible time began. Between 1933 and 1945 the world experienced a most extreme form of organised violence directed at the Jewish people, amongst others. The German leader, Hitler, and his followers, the Nazis, tried to wipe out every trace of Jews in the countries that they overran. Out of 10 million European Jews, about 6 million were murdered. The rest fled. This time is known as the Holocaust.

After the Holocaust, the movement for Jews to have a country of their own grew stronger. The State of Israel

was set up. Today Jews world-wide can claim Israeli citizenship.

Many of the people who were living in the area of Israel fled to neighbouring Arab countries, fearing attack from the Jews. They now wish to return to their lands, one of the reasons for the continuing hostility between Israel and her Arab neighbours. All sides continue to struggle for peace.

Israel tries to welcome every Jewish immigrant that wishes to come.

GLOSSARY

Ark originally the container used to keep the Ten Commandments safe during the Exodus. Every synagogue has an Ark, usually an ornate cupboard, in which the Torah scrolls are kept.

Ashkenazic basic synagogue traditions and practices of Jews who originated in Central, Eastern and Western Europe, and their descendants.

Bimah the platform in the synagogue, used for prayer.

Chassidim refers to mystical Orthodox Jews.

Exodus leaving slavery in Egypt and the period of forty years when the Jewish tribes survived in the desert until they were able to enter the Promised Land.

Diaspora Jews who have been scattered and live outside Israel.

Hebrew the language used since earliest times by the Jews for prayer. Official language of the State of Israel.

Holocaust Latin word meaning 'burning'. Jews use the word 'Shoah' which means destruction. The Holocaust refers specifically to the Nazi atrocities against Jews in the 1930s and 1940s.

Kosher food (and anything else) that is in line with Jewish laws.

Ner Tamid permanent light in the synagogue in front of the Ark.

Rabbi a teacher and counsellor who helps other Jews understand the Torah, and to deal with any other problems.

Sephardic basic synagogue traditions and practices of Jews who originated around the Mediterranean coast, and the East, and their descendents.

Shabbat day of rest: Friday sundown to Saturday nightfall.

Shema the major declaration of belief for Jews.

Skullcap the small circular headcovering worn as a sign of respect for God.

Synagogue (shul) a place for prayer and study, a meeting place for the community and for celebrations

Tallit prayer shawl worn in the synagogue.

Temple this was the most holy centre of worship in Jerusalem, destroyed before the end of the Roman era.

Torah the five books of Moses, plus commentaries. Means 'teaching' in Hebrew.

INDEX

Abraham 7
anti-semitism 30-1
Arabs 6, 31
Ark of the Covenant 10, 13

Babylonians 10
Bar Mitzvah/Bat Mitzvah 20, 21
Bible 7, 8, 15
Brit Milah 20

calendar 23
cemeteries 22
ceremonies 20-2
challah bread 18,19
Chanukah 26-7
charity 16
Chassidic Jews 5
cheder 15
children 4, 15, 17, 20, 21, 28, 29
circumcision 20
clothes 5, 14, 28

death, customs at 22
Diaspora 30
dress 5, 14, 28
duties 16-17

education 13, 15, 17

Egypt, Israelites in 7, 23, 25, 28-9
emigration 5, 6, 30

festivals 4, 23-9
foods 13, 17, 18, 26, 28-9

Haman 28
Hebrew language 4, 6, 8, 13, 15, 20
Holocaust, the 30, 31

Israel 7, 10, 30
        modern State of 5, 6, 31

Jerusalem 6, 11, 12, 25
Jesus of Nazareth 8

kosher foods 13, 17

Maccabees 26
marriage 21
Messiah, the 8, 11
minyan 13
mitzvot 16
Moses 7, 9, 10
mourning 22

Nazis 30, 31

observant Jews 16
Old Testament 8

Othodox Jews 12, 13

Palestine 31
Pesach (Passover) 23, 28-9
prayers 4, 11, 12, 14, 15, 16, 23
        for the dead 22
        Kiddush 18
Progressive Jews 12
Purim 28

rabbis 13, 14, 15, 20
Reform Jews 12, 13
Rosh Hashanah 23, 24

Seder meals 29
Shabbat, keeping the 18
Shema prayer, the 4, 15
Siddur (prayer book) 14
Sukkot 25
synagogues 5, 12-14

tallit 14
Temple, the 10-11, 13, 26
Ten Commandments 9, 10
tephillin 14